Original title:
Desert Rose Duet

Copyright © 2025 Creative Arts Management OÜ
All rights reserved.

Author: Fiona Harrington
ISBN HARDBACK: 978-1-80566-768-1
ISBN PAPERBACK: 978-1-80566-838-1

Unfolding Near the Oasis

In the sand, we chase our dreams,
With camels dressed in silly schemes.
A mirage leads us, oh so sly,
We laugh as we wave goodbye.

Sipping tea while the sun glares bright,
Our shadows dance, a comical sight.
A cactus winks, it seems to say,
'Hello, friend! Why not stay and play?'

We throw a party with dates and sand,
Inviting lizards, what a band!
The lizards groove, the sun keeps beat,
In this wild place, life feels so sweet.

As night unfolds, the stars appear,
We toast to laughter, sip our beer.
Under a moon that starts to glow,
We sing our song with a twinkly show.

A Lament in the Sun

Oh, the heat, it makes us sweat,
A hefty price for laughter, yet.
We try to dance, but trip on sand,
A graceful fall, unplanned and grand!

The sun above, it shines so bold,
As we concoct tales of gold.
Prickly pears? We dare to taste,
A fruit fight? Oh, what a waste!

With flip-flops on, we start to glide,
But even those can't save my pride.
I take a dive, right in the dunes,
A poofy cloud that plays the goon!

A cacti choir sings out loud,
Their prickly tone draws quite a crowd.
We laugh and sing, while losing track,
In this jest, there's no looking back.

Two Hearts in Bloom

In a land where cacti dance,
Two hearts collide in a silly prance.
With laughter ringing through the sand,
They twirl like they were BFFs, hand in hand.

A tumbleweed rolls by with flair,
Joining the couple in their affair.
They sip sweet tea under a sun so bright,
Are they dreaming? Oh, what a sight!

Dance of the Dunes

The dunes shimmy like they've got a groove,
While our duo makes their clumsy move.
Sand flies high with every twirl,
Feel the rhythm in this sandy whirl.

A tumble here, a trip over there,
Laughter echoes, tickling the air.
With a hat that's lost on a gusty breeze,
They spin and giggle with effortless ease.

Parched Palette

Paint splatters on a canvas of sand,
Two artists in tow, plotting their grand plan.
With colors that clash like a wild storm,
They create a mess that's slightly out of norm.

Sipping cactus juice, they squint at the sun,
Mixing their hues, oh what a run!
A masterpiece smudged with a splash and a splatter,
Who knew art could come from such silly chatter?

Velvet Petals and Grit

With petals soft but grit in their bones,
They weave through the flowers, avoiding the stones.
A sunburnt nose and mismatched shoes,
These two are the kings of the silly blues.

They skedaddle past lizards with plenty of sass,
Racing to see who's the first to pass.
Velvet petals dance in the dusty breeze,
Who knew laughter could flourish with such ease?

Union of Opposites

In the sun, a cactus grinned,
While a bunny hopped in, unpinned.
"Why so prickly?" it did jest,
"Just keeping life a bit of a test!"

A shady vale where lilies cry,
"Why's the sun so shy to fly?"
The sand replied, with a light scoff,
"Because of all the heat I'm off!"

Petal Shadows at Twilight

Petals danced in evening's hue,
Beneath a sky, all pink and blue.
A butterfly, with swagger grand,
Said, "I'm the best in this whole land!"

But daisies laughed, with heads held high,
"Your tricks won't work, you silly fly!"
As shadows stretched, the flowers pranced,
In twilight's glow, they all just danced.

Nomadic Echo

Echoes bounce from rock to air,
A tumbleweed gave its own glare.
"Why roam around with no set goal?"
Said the wanderer, with a cheeky toll.

"Life's a jest, a funhouse spin,
I chase the whispers on the wind!"
The cactus rolled its weary eyes,
"Just don't ask me to sympathize!"

Embrace of the East Winds

East winds blew with a quirky smile,
Tickling palms for quite a while.
"Are you lost?" a squirrel did squeak,
"Just looking for my next intrigue!"

The winds replied with a playful pout,
"Fun's the aim, without a doubt! "
While lizards laughed on sunbaked stones,
"No worries here, we're not alone!"

Serene Soliloquy

In a land of sand and jest,
A cactus wore a fancy vest.
He summoned lizards for a dance,
While camels giggled; what a chance!

The sunbeams played a guessing game,
Who could sizzle, who would flame?
Between the dunes, a loud parade,
As tumbleweeds partied, unafraid!

Bees buzzed in a conga line,
While flowers sent a cheeky sign.
"Come join us for a silly feast!"
And even lizards danced at least!

Amidst the mirage, laughter soared,
Sandcastles built with humor stored.
In this oasis, all were bold,
With jokes aplenty, tales retold!

Tantalizing Horizons

Upon the winds, a whisper flew,
A mirage of a giant shoe.
A witty crow claimed it was gold,
Even his shadow laughed, so bold!

The horizon shimmered with delight,
As sunbeams danced with sheer delight.
With every step, they'd trip and fall,
Their laughter echoed, one and all!

A lizard donned a sombrero wide,
Claiming to be the desert's guide.
"Follow me," he said with flair,
"Or go in circles, if you dare!"

With pockets full of sunshine bright,
They strolled beneath the moonlit night.
In every grain, a story spun,
As sand-whirls laughed, all having fun!

Sunkissed Promises

In a field where cacti roam,
Two flowers made a quirky home.
They promised to be bright and bold,
While making jokes both hot and cold.

"Why'd the bee sit on my head?"
"One more pun, he'll surely dread!"
Their petals twirled, like dancing queens,
While shady squirrels peeked from between.

A sandstorm swept through with a laugh,
As cacti tried to take a bath.
"Wet feet are fun," a lizard said,
With muddy paws, he struck a pose instead!

Under the sun, their colors bloomed,
Each sunny joke perfectly tuned.
With promises that never faded,
In their laughter, joy cascaded!

Silent Rhapsody

Underneath that star-lit sky,
A sneaky snake gave sunbaths a try.
With shades so cool, he sipped some tea,
"A quiet life? No, not for me!"

Lizards rolled in the golden sand,
Practicing moves for their big band.
"Can't catch us!" they cheered and dashed,
With snakes nearby uncomfortably crashed.

Each grain hummed a melody sweet,
While nature's giggles led the beat.
In silent rhapsody they swayed,
No undercurrents, just fun displayed!

When night fell, the stars played tricks,
Dancing by with magic flicks.
With every twinkle, laughter soared,
In desert dreams, all were adored!

Petals Against a Sandstorm

In a whirlwind of blossoms, we twirl,
Dust bunnies join in, an unexpected swirl.
The cacti chuckle, a prickly parade,
As petals fly high in a comical cascade.

Oh, how we dance, dodging gusts galore,
With seeds in our hair, we giggle and roar.
Winds tease our laughter, a riot to see,
A storm of petunias, just you and me.

Lullabies Beneath the Sun

Sung to the rhythm of sunbeams that play,
Silly serenades drift in the heat of the day.
A cactus hums softly, tapping its toes,
While bumblebees buzz in ridiculous rows.

We sway to the tune of a lopsided hat,
As laughter erupts from a sneaky little rat.
With shadows so long on the warm sandy ground,
Our giggles collide, making mirth all around.

Sands Between Us

In the sway of the dunes, we tumble and slide,
With each grain of sand, a secret we hide.
We build silly castles, then watch them all fall,
The tide of our laughter outshines it all.

Like hermit crabs scuttling, we search for our shade,
With sunscreen slapped on like a parade.
The grains in our shoes and the joy in our hearts,
Each moment together, a comedy starts.

Whispering Cacti

The cacti lean in to share their best jokes,
Telling tales of tall tales and dreamy blokes.
They rattle their spines, like a comical band,
As we sip on our drinks, feeling quite grand.

A cactus winks, with a spiky grin wide,
As tumbleweed rolls past, a fun little ride.
In a desert so vast, with laughter galore,
We find our own rhythm, we couldn't ask more.

Mirage of Togetherness

In the sand, two shadows dance,
Chasing dreams with a goofy prance.
One finds a lizard, the other a shoe,
Laughing all day, just us two.

With a sip of cactus juice, we toast,
To the silly things we love the most.
A mirage of partners, lost in the scene,
Finding joy in places unseen.

Bloom in the Arid

Petals pop up like jokes in the heat,
Who knew cacti could dance on their feet?
We giggle at blooms, so bright and absurd,
In this arid land, it's the strangest word.

With every prick, we laugh and we play,
Fluffy flowers in shades of dismay.
Two clowns in hats of desert delight,
Chasing laughter under the bright sunlight.

Harmony in Dunes

On the crest of a hill, we sing out loud,
Echoes of laughter, drawing a crowd.
A tumbleweed rolls, so wild with its tune,
Together we sway, like flowers in June.

The sun winks down, keeping time with our cheer,
Footprints in sand, a map of our year.
In this sandy ballet, we twirl and we spin,
Who knew that chaos could feel like a win?

Sunlit Blooms

Under the sun, our hats fly away,
Giggling together in a bright, silly sway.
Sunlit blooms nod, they join the fanfare,
Dancing absurdly, without a care.

Laughter erupts like a well-timed pun,
In this bizarre garden, we're always the fun.
We chase the mirage of laughter and light,
Growing together, what a delight!

Cadence in the Sand

A cactus winks in the daylight,
With shadows dancing on the ground.
Two roadrunners plot a high flight,
While lizards jiggle all around.

The sun throws parties on the dunes,
While tumbleweeds try to join in.
A jackrabbit hums cartoon tunes,
As mirage pools giggle and spin.

Sandcastles rise like silly dreams,
Each grain a story to be told.
They tumble in the heat, it seems,
While seagulls try to break the mold.

A lizards' band plays desert blues,
With rattlesnake slicing the groove.
Both tortoises and coyotes snooze,
In the warmth, they find their move.

Layers of Time and Bloom

Under layers of sassy sun,
The cacti gather quite the crowd.
They poke and prod, then grin and run,
Like they're comedians, proud.

The flowers giggle in the breeze,
Their colors swapping silly tales.
They sway like dancers, light and free,
While honeybees lose all their sails.

A tumbleweed starts a conga line,
As the sun begins to set.
With every twist, a punchline,
Making sure no one forgets.

The moon sneaks in, awfully sly,
Winks at the party going strong.
In shadows, the critters laugh and sigh,
In this sandy world, everyone belongs.

Celestial Dances Among Cacti

Stars twinkle like cheeky sprites,
While cacti sway beneath the dark.
A scorpion dreams of frosty nights,
As owls hoot odd remarks.

Meteor showers sprinkle jokes,
As the universe laughs, so bright.
A cholla cactus proudly pokes,
Saying, 'Ain't I a pretty sight?'

The lizards bust all kinds of moves,
Kangaroo rats join in the show.
In this dance, it groves and grooves,
Beneath a moonlight's gentle glow.

Stars in the sky hum desert tunes,
While prickly plants sway side to side.
The night is filled with whims and dunes,
As all nature's creatures laugh and glide.

Starlit Brush with Thorns

In the stillness, thorns play tricks,
While night unfolds its wink and grin.
A nocturnal cabaret, it flicks,
As the critters softly spin.

The owls exchange gossip and laughs,
Each tale taller than the last.
In the brush, mischief crafts,
As shadows dance, bold and fast.

A jackrabbit leaps, a big ol' bound,
But lands on a pillow of prickly spines.
With a yelp, he twirls 'round and round,
Bouncing back with one of a kind signs!

The stars above chuckle and cheer,
As a lizard struts with a wink.
In this wild fest, there's never a fear,
Just laughter on sands that clink.

Petal and Stone

A petal danced upon the breeze,
It tickled a cactus with such ease,
The stone just chuckled, looking wise,
"You'll never catch me - I'm not so spry!"

But wait, that petal gave a spin,
And flung some dust upon the grin,
The stone now grimaced with dismay,
"Why make a mess? It's a sunny day!"

The sun laughed loud and lit the scene,
As prickly jokes turned quite routine,
Each giggle broke through desert's hum,
A pun-filled path for them to run.

So if you roam through sands so grand,
Look for the dance, take time to stand,
For petals and stones might just collide,
In a duet of laughs that won't subside.

Harmonies of the Hidden Oasis

In a secret spot where shadows play,
A lizard crooned, in a quirky way,
To palm trees swaying, all out of tune,
Maracas made from a plastic spoon!

A cactus joined in, his needles pricked,
"Your rhythm's fine, but it's quite a trick!"
The lizard winked, danced with a twist,
"It's a hidden jam; it can't be missed!"

The oasis giggled, splashing around,
Echoes of laughter were joyfully found,
A chorus rose from the bright, warm sand,
As friends enjoyed their impromptu band.

So when you think the heat is dire,
Tune into nature; it will conspire,
For harmony lives where none can see,
Underneath the date palm's jubilee!

Sunbeams in the Arid Expanse

The sunbeams leaped on the golden dunes,
Chasing shadows like playful raccoons,
A tumbleweed twirled with all its might,
"Hey, keep up! You're dragging, that's not right!"

A saguaro sighed, with arms spread wide,
"These sunbeam races? They take my pride!"
But then the sun winked, its warmth embraced,
"Just smile and glide; we all love the chase!"

A lizard zipped by, quite full of glee,
"Catch me if you can! Oh, can't you see?"
The sunbeams shrieked, "We'll never tire!"
And danced till they spun in tireless fire!

In the arid expanse, where the mirage lies,
Laughter and light painted bluer skies,
So join the race, if you dare, my friend,
For in this sunbeam fun, there's no end!

The Fragrance of Memory

A whiff of spice in the spicy air,
Said a sagebrush plant with stories to share,
"I once was a chef with a dire red stain,
Now I just season the desert rain!"

A tumbleweed joined with a flourish and flip,
"Last week I rolled into a pizza strip!"
The sagebrush laughed till it nearly cried,
"Who knew that the winds could glide and decide?"

The shadows whispered of days gone by,
Of picnics and boots that climbed so high,
In the fragrance of memory, laughter bloomed,
As wildflower dreams recycled and zoomed!

So when you wander through sands of lore,
Breathe in the tales of the desert floor,
For every scent tells a story, you see,
In the fragrant past, we're forever free!

Whispers of the Cacti

In a land where shadows sway,
The cacti gossip every day.
Prickly jokes they love to share,
While tumbleweeds dance without a care.

A cactus winks, a lizard grins,
As the sunburnt laughter begins.
Sipping water from a teacup,
They toast to life, never giving up.

Dune Serenade

The dunes sing a silly tune,
With grains of sand that mock the moon.
A mirage of a dancing bear,
Leaves onlookers gasping in despair.

While lizards wear their finest hats,
And sunbaked minds get lost in chats.
A fleeting breeze, a giggling rush,
As nature's jesters play in hush.

Sunlit Petals in Arid Lands

Petals laugh in the blazing sun,
Declaring desert life is fun.
A bloom bursts forth with cheeky flair,
While rock formations stop and stare.

They throw their seeds like happy confetti,
While bees buzz by, feeling quite petty.
A rumble of laughter fills the air,
Nature's antics everywhere.

Love Among Shifting Sands

Two coyotes share a romantic meal,
On a dish of critters, what a deal!
While cacti shake their wise old heads,
At how romance blooms on warm beds.

The shifting sands play matchmaker,
Stirring up love, like a troublemaker.
Under the stars, they howl with glee,
In the wild, they're wild and free.

Passion in the Parched

In a land where cacti wear crowns,
A lizard dances in silly gowns.
Sandstorms come with a feathery touch,
Who knew dry dirt could tickle so much?

Lizards slide on their tiny feet,
Hiding from sun like it's a big treat.
Watermelons grow on cactus trees,
But only if the wind says, "Please!"

A cactus grand ball, the invitation's a joke,
With all the lizards laughing, they croak.
"Please, no thorny pricks on my arm,"
They laugh 'til they dance, no cause for alarm.

After the show, the sun waves goodnight,
And all the lizards call it a night.
In the twilight's embrace, they break out in song,
Where the land is dry, but the laughter is strong!

Harmonious Horizons

In a heatwave where the mirage reigns,
A band of cacti plays the plains.
With rattlesnake rhythm, they strum along,
While the tumbleweeds hum a silly song.

A bluebird arrives, looking for fun,
Joined the jam under the scorching sun.
He forgot his shades, but found a wide grin,
As he jigged with the tunes, he forgot the sin.

The sun winks down, a punny prank,
While shadows dance on the sandy bank.
A giraffe tries to shimmy, but loses the beat,
Falls on his neck; the crowd can't be beat.

In this desert gig on a stage of clay,
The laughter spills out, there's no better way.
With each cheery note beneath the blue sky,
The horizon laughs back, as toes tap high!

Song of the High Sun

Oh, the sun sings loud in the noonday heat,
With a voice so bright, it tickles your feet.
It beckons coyotes to join in the fun,
Even the prickly pears try to run.

A sand dune just giggled, it rolled down a hill,
While cactus critters practiced their skill.
The sun called them over, "Let's all have a cheer,
For the shallower graves of the lost cactus peers!"

The audience swayed in the breeze so warm,
Ants carried watermelons; what a bizarre charm.
The dance-offs erupted in the golden glow,
Where spiky companions put on quite the show.

With laughter that echoed through the bright, barren land,

Nature united, an improbable band.
Under that brazen sky, they all found their place,
In a melody woven with humor and grace!

Bound by Blossoms

In a garden of dust, where blooms seldom grow,
Two flowers laughed loudly, put on quite the show.
"I'm prettier than you!" sang the rose with flair,
The lily replied, "But I have more hair!"

Caught in a quarrel, they danced all around,
Entwined like a vine, they spun off the ground.
"Let's bet who lasts longer, baked in the sun!"
"I'm more than just pretty; I'm here for the fun!"

A breeze swooped down, both flowers took flight,
Swaying on petals, they twirled in delight.
With giggles and tickles from the warm, sunny glow,
They realized their bond was the best one to grow.

So arm in arm, they basked in the cheer,
Among all the critters that came drawing near.
In this hilarious tangle, as friends they din,
Proving that laughter can always begin!

The Thorned Embrace

In a garden of prickles, we found our fun,
Laughing at thorns, under the blazing sun.
You tickle my petals, I poke at your side,
In this silly ballet, we take a wild ride.

With arms full of laughter, we dance in delight,
Two cacti in costumes, a comical sight.
We hug and we stumble, both happy and sore,
In this prickly romance, we laugh and explore.

Mirage of Two Hearts

In a shimmering heatwave, we chase after dreams,
Like mirages that waltz, or so it seems.
You wink, I blush, and we're lost in the haze,
Our hearts do the cha-cha, in a whimsical daze.

With silly confessions that sparkle and shine,
We dance under stars, sipping sweet desert wine.
Fickle and funny, our love is a game,
In this mirage of mischief, we're never the same.

Blooming in Barren Beauty

In a land with no flowers, we giggle and grin,
Two odd little buds, that's where we begin.
With laughter like petals, we thrive in the sand,
In this barren wild place, we make quite a stand.

You sprout little jokes, while I blossom with glee,
In this awkward duet, just you and me.
When life gives us prickles, we fashion them bright,
Blooming together, our spirits take flight.

Oasis of Secrets

In a hidden away spot, where laughter is free,
We sip on sweet secrets, just you and me.
With giggles like water, and chatter like breeze,
In our oasis of joy, we do as we please.

Your smile's a sunbeam, it twinkles and skips,
As we toast to the moments with funny little quips.
With jokes in the air, and sand at our toes,
In this warm little haven, our silliness grows.

Serenade of Solitude

In a land where cacti sway,
The lizard dances, come what may.
With spiny friends, they form a band,
Strumming tunes in sandy land.

A tumbleweed rolls by with flair,
It tips its hat, without a care.
The sun plays tricks, it seems to glow,
While I just laugh at this wild show.

A rattlesnake's a funny chap,
He rattles jokes while taking a nap.
In this lonely, quirky place,
I find joy in this dry embrace.

So here I stand, with cactus kin,
In this oddball world, I can't help grinning.
With desert breeze and laughter loud,
Solitude's turned into a crowd.

Whispers of the Yucca

The yucca plant, a sage so wise,
It whispers secrets 'neath the skies.
I swear I heard it crack a joke,
About the cactus and his cloak.

A cactus winks, a sly old sprite,
In the bright sun, they share delight.
While tumbleweeds join in the fun,
They roll and tumble, just on the run.

A jackrabbit hops with style and grace,
Chasing shadows in this warm place.
With yucca's laughter swirling near,
Beneath the sun, we've nothing to fear.

So let us dance and sing a tune,
With silly moves beneath the moon.
For in this land so dry yet bright,
Whispers tell of pure delight.

Balanced Between Thorn and Tenderness

Among the thorns, there blooms a rose,
In prickly hugs, sheer joy bestows.
A little bug just took a dive,
Sipping sweet nectar, feeling alive.

A hedgehog stands, a spiky guy,
With dreams of flight, he wants to fly.
"I'll ride a hawk!" he shouts with glee,
But just ends up stuck in a tree.

The sun dips low, the shadows play,
A flower's blush, it turns to gray.
Yet laughter bubbles, fills the air,
For life gives thorns, yet we do care.

So here's to those, both thorn and bloom,
In this odd dance, we find our room.
With every giggle, we'll persist,
In a world where none can resist.

Twilight Flowers in Parched Hues

As twilight whispers, colors shift,
In parched hues, nature gives a gift.
A cactus giggles, bends in mirth,
At the comedy of this dry earth.

The javelina joins, boots in the sand,
Attempting to dance, it's quite unplanned.
With squeals and snorts, they sway and bounce,
In this dusty frontier, laughter pounces.

Pale moonlight glints on spiky crowns,
As shrubby dancers wear their frowns.
Yet in this quirky, sun-soaked space,
Each stumble is met with warm embrace.

So let's toast to the twilight blooms,
Underneath the stars, laughter looms.
In every cactus, in every jest,
In desert nights, we are truly blessed.

Swaying Shadows at Dusk

In the breeze, shadows tease,
Dancing heads in silly ease.
Cacti wobble, plants rejoice,
Even tumbleweeds have a voice.

Lizards laugh, they take a chance,
In their very clumsy dance.
Sunset's glow makes us all grin,
A cheeky show, let's jump in.

The mirage sparkles like a joke,
Even the dry weeds start to poke.
Funny hats on cactus tall,
A wild party, come one, come all!

As the day ends, laughter swells,
In the night, we hear the bells.
With every sway, the fun unfolds,
In the dusk, pure joy behold.

Souls Entwined in Dry Winds

In a land where hot winds sigh,
Two gophers plot, oh my, oh my!
Bouncing feet on dry, cracked ground,
In their world, fun's always found.

Across the dunes, a tale is spun,
A tumbleball that's just for fun.
Chasing shadows like a game,
In this heat, they stake their claim.

A sprinkle of sand flies around,
Giggling creatures make no sound.
With the breeze, they twist and twirl,
Happiest duo in a whirl.

As sunset paints the sky so bright,
The sand-dancers leap with delight.
In this arid land of jest,
Friendship reigns, they love it best.

Dance of the Sun-Kissed Blooms

Flower hats upon their heads,
In the sun, they make their beds.
Swaying, giggling, bright and bold,
Tales of blooms, a joy retold.

Petals flutter in wild delight,
Basking in the warm sunlight.
Bees are buzzing, joining the fun,
In the garden, everyone's spun.

A bloomin' ballet, oh so grand,
Dance of petals, oh, aren't they grand?
With every move, each color shines,
Nature's laughter, perfectly aligns.

As night approaches, they take a bow,
Under stars, they dance somehow.
Sun-kissed blooms in moonlight's grip,
Together in joy, they brightly skip.

Echoes of a Parched Garden

In the garden, echoes play,
Plants whisper secrets all day.
With dry leaves shaking, joy takes flight,
In the stillness, laughter's bright.

Plants gossip under the pale moon,
Roses cheer with a funny tune.
Daffodils gossip, bolstered joy,
Even sage cracks jokes, oh boy!

The soil, cracked, wears a grin,
As the old cactus chimes in.
Ticklish roots and shying vines,
Create a dance of silly lines.

As dusk settles, laughter soars,
In this dry land, joy restores.
Parched garden filled with a jest,
In the echoes, humor's best.

Starlit Serenade

Under the stars, we dance like fools,
Twinkling lights, breaking all the rules.
A cactus in heels, oh what a sight,
Laughing so hard, we forget the night.

Singing to lizards, their heads will sway,
One strummed guitar, just leads us astray.
Jumping on dunes as if they're a stage,
A tumble here and there, it's all the rage.

The moon takes notes of our goofy stance,
A mirage joins in, oh what a chance!
Fallen palm trees will witness our glees,
As tumbleweeds roll with the desert breeze.

With every hiccup, the stars burst out,
There's nothing more funny than our old clout.
Under a sky that dances in jest,
We're the best duo, that's just how we jest.

Windswept Whispers

Whispers of wind, they giggle and tease,
What's that noise? Oh it's just the bees!
A tumbleweed strolls with a jaunty flair,
Waving its branches, saying, 'Catch me if you dare!'

Sand in our boots, we waddle in style,
Every step taken, a new funny trial.
A pair of sunglasses on a big old rock,
This place is a fashion, but still we mock.

A mirage appears, it's my long-lost twin,
We laugh so hard, we must have been kin.
Chasing our shadows as they break free,
What a wild scene, a hilarious spree!

Oh winds, they blow with a "whoosh" and "whirr,"
While the sun takes selfies, oh what a blur!
In this crazy land, we just can't resist,
Every gust of laughter is a thing not to miss.

Echoes of the Sirocco

The swirling winds call with a giggle and glee,
Who knew they'd sound like a raucous marquee?
Every footstep falls with a puff and a pop,
As we leap through the dunes, we just can't stop.

"Hey, watch your hair!" yells my friend with a flair,
It's a wild style now, who needs a haircare?
We invent new dances, spinning with grace,
But end up tripping, that's the comical race.

Sirocco plays tricks like a seasoned clown,
Turning our frowns upside down.
Let's wear our hats backwards, what a delight,
In this sandy circus, everything's bright.

Echoes of laughter ripple through the night,
Even the cacti seem to take flight.
With every wild joke, we plant our roots deep,
In this land of hilarity, our hearts take a leap.

Lush in the Barren

In this barren land, we bring the cheer,
Who knew that laughter would thrive here?
A fountain of fun where the dry winds blow,
Making jokes with the cacti, just putting on a show.

A rogue tumbleweed dances, oh what a tease,
We can't help but giggle at how it flees.
Each joke like a cactus, prickly yet kind,
With memories blooming, we're hilariously entwined.

Tables of mirages serve coffee and cakes,
We raise a toast with our silly mistakes.
Under the sun, our spirits will soar,
Even in barren, we find so much more.

So here's to the laughter, with sand in our toes,
A lush celebration wherever it goes.
In this quirky land, all that we see,
Is fun in the barren, wild and carefree.

Spirited Under the Sun

In the heat, we dance so bright,
Chasing shadows, what a sight!
Lizards laugh as they zoom by,
We wear hats like floppy pies.

Sipping juice with silly straws,
Cacti giggle, it's applause!
With each step, the sand does squeak,
Can you hear the tumbleweed speak?

Flipping pancakes on the grill,
One lands on my friend's head, still!
Sunburned cheeks and silly grins,
We twirl like dancers on a spin.

Laughter echoes, fills the air,
Seagulls join, say "Do you dare?"
With the sun as our best mate,
We won't stop; it's way too late.

Sun-Kissed Whimsy

Underneath the beaming sun,
We play tricks; it's so much fun!
Camel rides with lopsided seats,
We giggle at our sandy feats.

Bouncing on a beach ball tall,
Stumbling like a penguin's call,
With flip-flops flapping on our toes,
We twirl and whirl like summer's prose.

Ice cream cones in crazy flavors,
Eat too fast, we'll need some savors!
Melting down our sticky hands,
A sticky mess that laughs and stands.

Jellyfish do the limbo dance,
We're all caught in a wobbly trance,
As we bask in sunshine gold,
Our funny tales will be retold.

Oasis of Our Hearts

In the shade, we sip cold tea,
Banter flies like bees, you see!
Palm trees wave, they ask for joy,
With every splash, like a bold ploy.

Turtles race in a silly game,
Who knew they'd bring such fame?
With our thirsts we gladly cheer,
Blowing bubbles, oh so dear!

Feathered friends in wacky hats,
Join our dance, what silly chats!
We strut like peacocks, just for grins,
While the world around us spins.

Wave your arms; let's serenade,
With our hearts in fun parade,
Underneath the twinkling stars,
We'll sing and laugh from near and far.

Untamed Duet

With a wink, we take the stage,
Silly songs at every age!
Dancing feet, we look absurd,
Now it's time for the next word!

Clouds above are cotton candy,
We sing loud; it's not too dandy!
The sun does shimmy, join the spree,
Together we find harmony.

Squirrels cheer and join the chase,
While cactus pricks hold a smart face.
To our tunes, the bugs all sway,
Creating laughter every day.

Together we laugh, no end in sight,
In this duet, pure delight!
With every note a funny twist,
We'll ride this wave; we simply insist.

Mirage of Our Dreams

In the sand, I see you dance,
But oh, it's just a chance.
A mirage, bright and coy,
Yet still, you bring me joy.

We chase shadows, wild and free,
In these dunes, just you and me.
With laughter echoing wide,
Pretend much, no need to hide.

Cacti wave as we sashay,
Underneath the sun's ballet.
Our laughter makes the sand sprawl,
In this heat, we'll have a ball!

So sip your cactus juice with class,
As time slips by, oh what a gas!
Dreams are bright, though grains may flake,
In mirage's grasp, we just can't break.

Fragrant Futures

Let's plant dreams on sandy soil,
With scents of laughter, free from toil.
A bouquet of hopes, let's intertwine,
Who knew the desert could smell so fine?

With visions blooming under the sun,
We'll sprout some giggles, just for fun.
A sip of laughter, a dash of cheer,
Fragrant futures draw us near.

We'll chase the sun, take silly flights,
In our own world, we'll set the sights.
A sprinkle of joy, a whiff of thrill,
Our fragrant futures, a sunny hill.

So grab your hat, we're on our way,
In this funny dance, we'll laugh and play.
With each bright bloom, we solidify,
Fragrant futures whispering, "Oh my!"

Poetry of the Parched

Words tumble like dust in the breeze,
Parched throat, I croak, but please!
Supplies low, but jokes run high,
In the heat, we simply fly!

With every quip, our spirits rise,
Like cacti blooming, oh what a surprise!
We sing to the stars, a wild charade,
In this thirst, funny thoughts invade.

Haikus in sand, we carve with glee,
Where dryness reigns, so does our spree.
Jokes like mirages, out of reach,
Yet here we stand, ready to preach!

In the poetry of this parched land,
We're the jokesters, a gleeful band.
So raise your glass of mirage-flavored air,
In the comedy of life, we find our share.

Heartstrings in the Heat

Strumming chords of mirth and play,
Under the blazing light of day.
Our hearts, a symphony bare,
In the heat, we dance without a care.

The sun laughs back at our twirls,
As we trip on sand, not pearls.
With each note, we weave our tales,
In this shimm'ring heat, we'll never pale.

So play the lute made of tumbleweeds,
In a land where humor grows like seeds.
We serenade the sands with glee,
Heartstrings strummed, wild and free.

In the warm embrace of this sunny plight,
Our funny vibes take to flight.
So join the laugh, let spirits rise,
In this warm dream, what a surprise!

Timeless Togetherness

In the garden where we giggle,
Two cacti dance, they wiggle.
A tumbleweed rolls by, oh dear!
They're swinging to music we can't hear.

Their spines may poke, yet they unite,
In a conga line under the moonlight.
With every step, they burst with cheer,
A prickly party, let's give a cheer!

With laughter ringing through the air,
The desert blooms, it's quite the affair.
Saguaro's got some moves so bold,
While cholla tells stories, oh how they're told!

Together they twirl, no need for shoes,
In their sandy dance, there's no way to lose.
The night is young, let's share a laugh,
In this kooky quandary, they find their path.

Gold and Green Convergence

A sagebrush munches on a sunny snack,
While tumbleweeds join the silly pack.
In a field of gold, they take a stand,
Kicking up dust, a whimsical band.

Cacti in shades of green and glee,
Competing in funny names, what could they be?
'Prickly Pete' and 'Spiny Sally' take the floor,
They've got talent; oh, they'll roar!

A teal horizon, the sun bows down,
As laughter rings out, there's no frown.
The desert's a stage, it's a sight to behold,
Gold and green spinning stories untold.

With chuckles and quirks, they share a tale,
Of wild adventures and a curious snail.
In their foolish frolics, the day is won,
Glimmers of joy in the setting sun.

Hope in Harshness

Out in the stretch where the sand baked bright,
Two silly blooms twirl in delight.
One's a mirage, the other quite real,
With dreams of water, they share a meal.

"I'm flowering!" cries out the old sage,
"Though my story's written on an ancient page!"
Laughter erupts in the sun's fierce glare,
These tough little sprites don't have a care.

With every gust, they sway and bend,
Embracing a warmth that will never end.
Cockatoos squawk, "Oh, what a sight!"
In a hearty dance through the oppressive light!

The rocks may tumble, the sun still shines,
Their goofball antics cross the lines.
In harshness found, they loop and twirl,
Spreading joy with every whirl.

Boundless Blooms

Petals pop out with a silly zing,
While wind-blown weeds start to sing.
With colors bright and an untamed flair,
They throw a bash without a care.

In a world so wide, they shimmy and sway,
Creating chaos, come join the fray!
They tickle the air with laughter galore,
Bouncing off rocks, 'Let's open the door!'

A jester-like flower leads the pack,
While others follow, no signs of lack.
Joyous companions in bloom and jest,
They spread their comedy, and it's the best!

So, let us gather and dance with ease,
With colors and whirls, we aim to please.
For boundless blooms bring forth delight,
In a garden of giggles, all feels right.

In the Shade of Thorns

In the shade where cacti lean,
Two friends plot a silly scene.
With floppy hats and drinks to share,
They laugh, forgetting all the care.

Lizards laugh at their bright attire,
While a tumbleweed rolls by, a choir.
They dance around a prickly bush,
While cacti blush in the desert hush.

One attempts a daring leap,
Into a pile of dirt so steep.
Oh the giggles, oh the sighs,
As sand flies up to meet the skies.

In this land of funky glares,
Life's a jest in prickled heirs.
So raise a glass of cactus juice,
To friendship's quirky, funny truce.

Serenade in the Sands

Beneath the stars, they grab guitars,
Soft notes float past the shining stars.
A serenade for lizards near,
As they sip on cactus beer.

One tries to sing a high note loud,
But the scorpions form a crowd.
They clap their claws, a humorous beat,
While a roadrunner taps his feet.

The sun shines down on sand dune hills,
Creating shadows, causing chills.
Each strum a laughter, each chord a cheer,
As the moon joins in, it draws near.

With every verse, they share a smile,
Amidst the cacti, life feels worthwhile.
For in these dunes where both compete,
They find the rhythm their hearts can meet.

Desert Dances

With scarves of colors, they twirl in glee,
Ignoring the brush of the prickly spree.
Each step a mix of sand and sweat,
In this wild dance, no signs of regret.

A tumbleweed competes to spin,
While they whack at flies with a grinning grin.
Laughter echoes through the barren land,
As they stumble on, not well-planned.

One trips on the edge of a sandy mound,
And face-plants onto the soft ground.
With giggles erupting like a desert bloom,
They shake off the dust, erase the gloom.

In the heat, their spirits stay bright,
Dancing shadows, filled with delight.
So let them sway till the morning dew,
For fun in the heat is what they do!

Synchronized Souls

In sync they prance across the dunes,
Like waltzing flowers, no time for tunes.
One waves a flag made of old kelp,
While they giggle and try not to yelp.

A mirage flickers, a funny sight,
As they leap forth in pure delight.
With arms outstretched like a cactus high,
They reach for the sun, almost fly.

But watch out for that sneaky breeze,
That sends their hats flying with ease.
They chase in circles, laughter grows,
As tumbleweeds join in their shows.

Two hearts beat in this sandy whirl,
Sharing chuckles, making life swirl.
In this duet of silly plays,
They find their joy in the sun's bright rays.

Secrets of the Oasis

Beneath the sun, we splash and play,
With camels thinking they own the day.
A jug of water spills with a splash,
Laughing at the sight, we make a dash.

The palm trees gossip, they lean and sway,
Whispers of secrets in the heat's ballet.
A cactus roll, oh what a sight,
Trying to dance, but oh, not quite!

Sand dunes giggle with every breeze,
As we stumble and tumble, brought to our knees.
The mirage teases, it's hard to discern,
Hot dogs or camels? It's our turn to learn!

In the oasis where laughter flows,
We discover friendship, that's how it grows.
With every sip from our lemony drink,
We toast to adventures, and laugh till we sink.

Shadows of Two Souls

Two shadows dance, oh what a sight,
Sipping our drinks under the moonlight.
We spot a tortoise, slow yet grand,
Who's stealing our snacks? Oh what a plan!

Our laughter echoes between the palms,
While trading tales that bring such charms.
Hot air balloons float, it's quite absurd,
We shout, 'Watch out!' but who's really heard?

The stars above wink, they join the fun,
As we slip on pebbles, it's how we run.
A game of hide and seek beneath the night,
Who knew shadows could bring such delight?

With every giggle, we light up the dark,
Sharing our secrets, igniting a spark.
In this silly dance of shadows, we find,
True friendship blossoms, intertwined.

Thorns and Petals

In a garden where thorns like to thrive,
Petals poke fun, oh they come alive!
A prickly joke tossed by a rose,
"Watch your step, buddy, it's thorny prose!"

We pick a bouquet, with giggles galore,
While dodging the thorns, oh it feels like war!
"Who knew flowers could be so rude?
A cactus is better, at least it's shrewd!"

The blooms all chuckle, bright in the sun,
As each little prick just adds to the fun.
"Let's have a tea party, come sit with us!
Just watch for the thorns — they tend to fuss!"

With laughter and petals scattered around,
In this wacky meadow, joy can be found.
Thorns may be sharp, but they can't steal
The laughter we share, it's the best deal!

Heartbeats under a Scorching Sun

Under the heat, we jump and skip,
With heartbeats racing, we start to trip.
The sun beats down, a relentless foe,
Yet laughter bubbles, it's how we flow.

Watermelons splatter, oh what a scene,
Sticky and sweet, we're living the dream.
Ice cream dreams turn into a race,
Till the melting mess leaves a sugary trace!

Our antics blur in the sun's bright glare,
As we chase shady spots, it's hardly fair!
"Why's the sun so high?" one friend cries,
We all just laugh; it's a recipe for pies!

In this hot dance with rays above,
Our hearts beat wildly, it's life that we love.
So here's to the fun, the heat, the bright,
Heartbeats in rhythm, all day and night.

Dunes of Desire

In the sands, we danced and tripped,
With every tumble, laughter zipped.
Sipping water, oh what a spree,
Who knew dry air could make us glee!

Camels glanced, as if to giggle,
While we played, just a little wiggle.
A mirage appeared, we chased with care,
Turns out it's just hot air, I swear!

Twilight in the Oasis

Under stars, we cracked some jokes,
While sipping juice, we felt like folks.
"Is that a mirage or just my drink?"
We laughed hard, not a moment to think.

The moonlit waves made shadows dance,
As we twirled, not leaving a chance.
What a sight, a cactus with flair,
Wishing on stars, giggling in the air!

Blossoms Beneath a Fiery Sky

Petals floated, we swatted flies,
In this heat, we sure looked wise.
Hats askew and clothes askew,
Who knew flowers could smell so askew?

We searched for shade, a daunting quest,
Found a lizard, he looked quite distressed.
"Join the party, be one of us!"
He blinked once, clearly nonplussed!

Heartbeats in the Heat

Our hearts raced under the blazing sun,
Each beat echoed, we were having fun.
"Don't you dare fall in a cactus, please!"
Laughter erupted, like a cooler breeze.

With every step, we made a friend,
Flies and toads, they'd never offend.
In this warmth, we found our groove,
Living it up, oh how we move!

A Flourish of Flame

In the heat of the sun, we dance and we sway,
With cactus in hand, we lost the bouquet.
A tumbleweed rolls, in the midst of our spree,
Who knew wildflowers could be so carefree?

A lizard plays tag on the back of my shoe,
While I sip cactus juice, oh how it's brand new!
With laughter and giggles, we prance in our zest,
Underneath all this chaos, we simply are blessed.

Our hats fly away, now they're caught in a tree,
Our shadows are laughing, just look and you'll see!
With petals in pockets, we're fashionably late,
To the party of prickles, we just call it fate.

As the sunset ignites, our arms start to glow,
We're twirling through fields where the wild breezes blow.
With friends by our side, and a punch-drunk refrain,
We flourish and flame, oh what a wild gain!

Embered Embrace

With a wink and a grin, we share a hot fry,
Under glaring sunlight, just you and I.
The tumbleweeds giggle, they know all the best,
Secrets of laughter put our hearts to the test.

You threw me a cactus, in jest, oh so mean,
But I laughed so hard, you should've seen the scene!
Together we sizzle in this silly affair,
A whirlwind of fun in the warm desert air.

Our shadows are stretched like old chewing gum,
While the sun plays peek-a-boo, oh, isn't it fun?
With odd little jokes that we can't help but share,
Each guffaw a spark in this wild love affair.

As night casts a cover, the stars blink their cheer,
We'll sit by the fire, with laughter so near.
In this embered embrace, our hearts do ignite,
With giggles as fuel, we'll light up the night!

Petals Beneath a Blazing Sky

Underneath the sun, where the funny things shrink,
We find joy in shadows, and laughter to drink.
With petals beneath, vibrant colors collide,
Two fools in the wild, with nothing to hide.

A band of coyotes join in on our fun,
Howling our tune, like a wild raucous run.
With sun hats so large, we could start a parade,
Lined up in a row, we are unafraid.

Our feet in the dust, as we scamper about,
You stepped on a flower, oh dear, what a clout!
But flowers forgive us, they giggle and sway,
As we twirl through the fields, like kids at play.

So cheers to the blooms, our spirits so spry,
With petals beneath us, we float 'neath the sky.
In this land of mirth, where the sunsets collide,
We're picking the petals, with hearts open wide!

The Bloom Between Us

In a field of confusion, we started a war,
With water balloon fights, yes, we've done it before!
Your laughter is music, as sweet as can be,
In this bloom between us, we're simply carefree.

The sun laughs so hard that it spills all its rays,
While we chase after shadows through silly displays.
With flowers as crowns and a smile that's wide,
Two clowns in a garden, we dance side by side.

A prickly remark, I toss in the breeze,
You retaliate swiftly, my heart starts to freeze!
But the bloom that we share, through the giggles and jest,

Turns the moments to magic, we know we are blessed.

As dusk settles in, and the stars share their light,
We sit in the grass, everything feels just right.
In this bloom between us, we'll cherish the cheer,
Two friends in the wild, to each other we're near.

Whispers of the Sand

The dunes they sway, oh what a sight,
As camels dance beneath the moonlight.
A critter skitters, oh what a show,
Sand in my pants—who put on this show?

A cactus grins, it thinks it's cool,
While I just trip, oh isn't life a fool?
With each grain stuck in my hair,
I ponder if it's a fashion affair!

The sun beats down, oh such a tease,
I take a sip, then spill my freeze!
Lizards laugh and waltz about,
In this sandy realm, there's never doubt!

So here I am, with grit for a crown,
A goofy king wearing a sandy gown.
The whispers of the sand, I swear,
Make all my worries vanish into air!

Beauty Amidst the Barren

Amidst the dry where beauty's rare,
A cactus blooms with such a flair.
A lizard struts, so proud and spry,
Yet trips on rocks—oh me, oh my!

The sun will bake my brains today,
I'm dreaming of a cool cabaret.
With mirage drinks that dance and sway,
My thirst for laughter holds the way!

A tumbleweed rolls with flair and scream,
It rolls right past, steals my ice cream!
But in this barren, sandy ground,
A chuckle's the best treasure found!

So raise a toast with air so hot,
To all the laughs that we forgot.
In a land where laughter's the real prize,
I'll trade my woes for silly skies!

Mirage of Affection

In twilight's glow, I see a face,
But it's just a rock in a silly place.
With hearts and dreams that float around,
My fondness grows for the parody found!

A hawk swoops down, oh what a thief,
He snatched my sandwich—bring me relief!
Yet as I sit, in silly despair,
I spot a squirrel with a turtleneck flair!

The stars above wink at me tight,
They brush off the sand, say, "What a night!"
Each sparkle laughs, a cosmic delight,
In this mirage, affection takes flight!

So let's not fret, it's all a charade,
For beneath this laughter, friendships are made.
In mirages, we find what we seek:
Laughter and love, let's take a sneak!

Fragrant Fantasies

With every step, the dust does swirl,
I pretend to waltz, a silly twirl.
But oh! The aroma, what a mix!
Of sage and nonsense, I've made a fix!

A tumbleweed joins the merry dance,
As I trip and fall—what a romanced chance!
The scent of humor fills the air,
With prickly jokes, life's not so bare!

The sun sets low, a golden hue,
My laughter echoes, oh how it grew!
As shadows play with giggles and cheer,
In fragrant fantasies, joy is near!

So here we sit, in sandy bliss,
With every chuckle and silly kiss.
Let's relish moments, wild and free,
For in this land, we just "be"!

Blossoms in the Wind

In the desert blooms a sight,
Cacti dance with all their might.
Lizards laugh, oh what a scene,
Lost in sand, they're quite the queen.

Tumbleweeds roll, a playful chase,
Join the fun, it's a wild race.
Wind whispers tricks, a secret tease,
Petals flutter, the heart agrees.

With each gust, the laughter grows,
Bouncing hues in nature's prose.
Silly shadows play tag around,
Joyful chaos, in dust they're found.

So let us twirl in sunlit cheer,
Joy's the crown, let's all draw near.
In this land of mirthful spins,
A quirky world where laughter wins.

Celebration of Resilience

A cactus stands against the sun,
With a grin, says, 'Life is fun!'
Through the storms and silly blights,
It wears its spines like party lights.

Lizards scurry, tugging tails,
Chasing dreams like wind-blown sails.
Each new dawn brings goofy grace,
In this hot and sandy place.

With every tumble, every fall,
They rise again, and have a ball.
For laughter blooms amid the heat,
Their spirit dances, can't be beat.

So raise a glass to those who thrive,
In a desert where we all contrive.
To find the joy in every test,
A celebration that feels the best.

Through Grit and Grace

Amidst the rocks, a smile sprout,
Determined in what life's about.
With every challenge, they crack a joke,
Graceful strength in the sun's soft cloak.

Sandy paths may try to trip,
But laughter's the best little script.
Cacti wink with a playful cheer,
Swaying, dancing, year to year.

The sun is bright, but humor's gold,
In sandy tales, their joy is bold.
Through grit they grow, no room for gloom,
In this wild land, they always bloom.

So lift a laugh, let spirits race,
In every twist, we find our place.
With grit and grace, we strut our stuff,
In the desert, life's just a bit rough.

Alpine Melodies in a Sandstorm

In a storm, where grains collide,
The melodies of chaos ride.
A yodel here, a boom there,
Nature giggles, filled with flair.

Dusty hills sing a zany tune,
Under the watch of a cartoon moon.
Little critters prance and sway,
Making up for the cloudy day.

Through the swirls the echoes fly,
As the sun dips low in the sky.
Alpine dreams in a sandy whirl,
A funny dance, a twirl and swirl.

So bring your laughs and join the show,
In this wild wind, let your heart glow.
For even storms can't steal the fun,
In the chaos, we're all one.

www.ingramcontent.com/pod-product-compliance
Lightning Source LLC
Chambersburg PA
CBHW072144200426
43209CB00051B/453